WELCOME TO THE GALAXY

My
name
is
EARTH

MY FIRST BOOK OF PLANETS

Amelia Sealey

EARTH

I am the planet you live on. I am the only planet with organic life. I am 4.5 billion years old. I complete one rotation around my own axis in 23 hours, 58 minutes and 4 seconds.

My
name
is
SUN

SUN

I am a star not a planet. I am found at the center of the Solar System. I am 99.86% of the Solar System mass. My light reaches you in around 8 minutes.

My
name
is
MERCURY

MERCURY

I am the closest planet to the sun. A year on my surface is 88 days. I am the smallest planet in the Solar System. I don't have any satellites or ring systems.

My

name

is

VENUS

VENUS

I am the hottest planet in the Solar System. I am the brightest. I have an active surface including volcanos. I spin the opposite direction on Earth.

My
name
is
MARS

MARS

I am red in color. I am the fourth planet from the sun. I have the highest mountain in the Solar System and a volcano named Olympus Mons.

My
name
is
JUPITER

JUPITER

I am covered in clouds and I am the fifth from the sun. I am the largest planet in the Solar System. My giant red spot is a ranging sandstorm.

My
name
is
SATURN

SATURN

I am brown in color. My outer rings are extremely thin. They are made of dust and icy chunks. I am the King of the Moons, having a total of 82 confirmed moons.

My

name

is

URANUS

URANUS

I am blue in color. Humans have named me the icy planet. I am the coldest planet in the Solar System. It is possible to see me with the naked eye.

My
name
is
NEPTUNE

NEPTUNE

I am blue in color just like Uranus. I have to many storms in my atmosphere. I am the furthest planet from the sun.

WE HOPE YOU ENJOYED IT

Hey there!!!

We hope you enjoyed our book. As a small family company, your feedback is very important to us. Please let us know how you like our book at:
believepublisher@gmail.com

Without your voice we don't exist!

Please, support us and leave a review!

Thank you!!!

Milton Keynes UK
Ingram Content Group UK Ltd.
UKHW021526230624
444613UK00021B/206